PE

PERFECT

PEACE

F. B. MEYER

ECS
MINISTRIES
The Word to the World

Peace, Perfect Peace
F. B. Meyer (1847 – 1929)

Copyright © 2007 ECS Ministries

ISBN 978-1-59387-064-5

Published by:
    ECS Ministries
    P.O. Box 1028
    Dubuque, IA 52004-1028
    www.ecsministries.org

Edited by ECS Ministries. Original edition, 1897.

Cover and Interior Design: Ragont Design, Barrington, Illinois

All Scripture quotations, unless otherwise indicated, are taken
from the *New King James Version*. Copyright © 1979, 1980,
1982 by Thomas Nelson, Inc. Used by permission. All rights
reserved.

Printed in the United States of America

Peace, perfect peace, in this dark world of sin:
The blood of Jesus whispers peace within.

Peace, perfect peace, by thronging duties pressed:
To do the will of Jesus, this is rest.

Peace, perfect peace, with sorrows surging round:
On Jesus' bosom nought but calm is found.

Peace, perfect peace, our future all unknown:
Jesus we know, and He is on the throne.

Peace, perfect peace, death shadowing us and ours:
Jesus has vanquished death and all its powers.

It is enough: earth's struggles soon shall cease,
And Jesus call us to heaven's perfect peace.

—E. H. BICKERSTETH

F. B. Meyer *1847 – 1929*

Frederick Brotherton Meyer was born in London, England in 1847 and grew up in a Christian home. He graduated from London University in 1869 and completed his theological training at Regents Park Baptist College. F. B. Meyer pastored a number of churches and also had an itinerant speaking ministry visiting, among other countries, Canada, South Africa and the United States. He died in 1929.

A devoted student of God's Word, he was the author of over 40 books, including Bible biographies, devotional commentaries, sermon volumes and expository works.

Charles Spurgeon said of him, "Meyer preaches as a man who has seen God face to face."

CONTENTS

One

PEACE, PERFECT PEACE!

*P*eace, perfect peace! What music there is in the words! The very mention of them fills the heart with longings that cry out for satisfaction, and will not be comforted. Sometimes, indeed, we may succeed in hushing them for a little, as a mother does a fretting child, but soon they will break out again with bitter and insatiable desire. Our nature sighs for rest, just as the ocean shell which, when placed to the ear, seems to sigh for the untroubled depths of its native home. There is peace in the silent depths of the ocean, which bend with such gentle tenderness over our fevered, troubled lives. There is peace in the repose of the unruffled waters of the mountain lake, sheltered from the winds by the giant cliffs that surround it. There is peace at the heart of the whirlwind that sweeps across the desert in its fury. The peace of a woodland dell, of a highland glen, of a summer landscape, all touch us. And is there no peace for us, whose nature is so vast, so composite, so wonderful?

There is. As Jacob lay dying in Egypt, he prophesied how Shiloh, the Peaceful One, the Peace-giver, would come to give peace to men (Genesis 49:10). Weary generations passed by and still He did not come, until at

length there stood among men One whose
outward life was full of sorrow and toil but
whose sweet, calm face mirrored the
unbroken peace that reigned within His
breast. He was the promised Peace-giver. He
had peace in Himself, for He said, "*My*
peace." He had the power of passing that
peace on to others, for He said, "My peace I
give to you." Why should not each reader of
these lines receive the peace which Jesus had
Himself and which He waits to give to every
longing and receptive heart?

A poor woman timidly asked the
gardener of a wealthy man's greenhouse if he
would sell her just one bunch of grapes for
her dying child. He gruffly threatened to
summon the police unless she quickly left the
place. But as she sadly turned away, she
heard a young voice call her back, bidding
her stay, asking her story, and insisting on her
having as many bunches as she could carry
away with her. When she offered her a few

pennies in return, she was met by the sweet, laughing answer, "No, my dear woman, this is my father's greenhouse. We don't *sell* grapes here, but we are very pleased to *give* them. Take them for your dying child." Similarly, Jesus *gives* His peace to all who need it. Receive His peace with open arms.

His peace is *perfect* (Isa. 26:3)

Unbroken by storms. Uninvaded by mundane cares. Unreached by the highest surges of sorrow. Unstained by the contaminating touch of sin. The very same peace that reigns in heaven, where all is perfect and complete.

His peace is *as a river* (Isa. 48:18)

The person who dwells on its banks in time of drought is well supplied with water. It flows at early dawn as he goes to his daily toil. It is there at the scorching noon. It is there when the stars shine, hushing him to sleep with the melody of its waves. When he was a child, he plucked flowers on its bank. And when his foot shall cease to tread its banks, his children's children shall come to drink its streams. Think, too, how it broadens and deepens and fills up in its onward journey from its source to the boundless, infinite sea. So may our peace abide and grow with our years.

His peace is *great* (Isa. 54:13)

The mountains may depart and the hills be removed, yet God's peace will abide. Its music is louder than the noise of the storm. Learn the lesson of the Lake of Galilee—that the peace which is in the heart of Jesus and which He gives to His own can quell the greatest wind that ever swept down the mountain ravine and spent itself on the writhing waters beneath. For when the

Master rose and rebuked the wind and said to the sea, "Peace, be still," the winds ceased and there was a great calm.

His peace is *compatible with much tribulation* (John 16:33)

If we never find our path dipping down into the sunless valley we may seriously question whether we have missed our way to the Celestial City. The road to the Mount of Ascension invariably passes through the shadowed Garden of Gethsemane, over the steep ascent of Calvary, and then down into the Garden of the Grave. "We must through many tribulations enter the kingdom of God" (Acts 14:22). But in the midst of it all, it is possible to be kept in unbroken peace like that which possessed the heart of Jesus and enabled Him to calmly work a miracle of healing amid the commotion of His arrest (John 22:51).

His peace *surpasses all understanding* (Phil. 4:7)

God's peace cannot be put into words. It defies analysis. It must be experienced to be understood. The thing most like it is the joy of a child in a secure home where love and wise nurture combine to supply all its need. But even that falls short of the glorious reality. "Eye has not seen, nor ear heard, nor have entered into the heart of man the things which God has prepared for those who love Him. But God has revealed them to us through His Spirit" (1 Cor. 2:9-10). This peace will guard our hearts and minds, going

back and forth like a sentry before a palace, keeping intruders from breaking in. O that we might be ever protected by a guardianship so helpful and watchful and invulnerable to attack!

There are a few conditions, however, that demand careful thought.

THE BASIS OF PEACE IS THE BLOOD OF CHRIST

"Having made peace through the blood of His cross" (Col. 1:20). We sometimes hear men speak of "making their peace with God," but that is wholly needless. Peace has already been made. When Jesus died on the cross, He did all that needed to be done, and all that could be done—so far as God was concerned—in order to bring peace to men. Nothing more is required except to lay aside fear and suspicion and to accept the peace that He now sweetly and freely offers. "God was in Christ, reconciling the world to

14

Himself, not imputing their trespasses to them. . . . Be reconciled" (2 Cor. 5:19-20).

There were many obstacles to our peace, but they have been entirely met and put out of the way. God's holy justice, which would pursue us with its drawn sword, can say nothing against us because it has been more vindicated in the death of the Son of God than it could have been in the damnation and ruin of the sin-cursed world. The broken law, which might press its claims, is silenced by the full and complete satisfaction rendered it in the obedience and death of the Law-giver Himself. Conscience, even with its long and bitter record of repeated sin, feels able to appropriate forgiveness without scruple or alarm because it understands that God can be just and yet justify the believer in Jesus. "Who is he who condemns? It is Christ who died, and furthermore is also risen, who is even at the right hand of God, who also makes intercession for us" (Rom. 8:34).

On the evening of His resurrection, our Lord entered through the unopened doors into the chamber where His disciples were cowering for fear of the Jews. His benediction, "Peace to you," fell on their ears and brought exceeding comfort. After He had so said, He showed them His hands and His side, fresh from the cross, with the marks of spear and nails, so that He stood in their midst like a lamb, "as it had been slain." Do you wonder that they were glad? The heart must always be glad when it learns that the sure basis of peace is in the blood shed on the cross. Rest on that precious blood. Make much of it. Remember that God sees it, even if you do not. Be sure that it pleads through the ages with undiminished efficacy. And be at peace.

THE METHOD OF PEACE IS BY FAITH IN GOD'S WORD

How many Christians miss God's peace because they look into their hearts to see how they *feel!* If they feel right and happy they are at peace. But if they are physically or emotionally sick they become sad, depressed, and restless. Peace has taken flight.

This will never do. Life is not meant to be one, long, tortuous journey. This is not the blessed life that Jesus came to give us. To live like this is indeed to miss the prize of our high calling and to cast discredit on His dear name. If you seek peace through emotions and feelings you will seek it in vain. It may arrive, but like an overnight guest it will not stay. It may visit you like a transient gleam over the hillside, but it will be only a tiny break between long leagues of cloud. There is a more excellent way. Take up the Bible, the Word of God *to you*. Turn to some of the texts that shine like brilliant stars in the midnight sky. Consider, for instance, the following verses. Concentrate your mind and

17

> "THE BLOOD OF JESUS CHRIST HIS SON CLEANSES US FROM ALL SIN."

heart upon their mighty meaning.

"He who *hears* My word, and *believes* in Him who sent Me has everlasting life, and shall not come into judgment, but has passed from death into life" (John 5:24).

"By Him everyone who *believes* is justified from all things" (Acts 13:39).

"The blood of Jesus Christ His Son cleanses us from *all* sin" (1 John 1:7).

What do these words mean? Can they mean anything less than they say? And if they are as they seem, is it not clear that he who *believes* stands before God as a reconciled, accepted, and beloved child?

What is it to believe?

To believe is to look up to Jesus as your personal Savior, handing over to Him the whole burden of your soul, for time and eternity. It is to be sure that He takes it at the moment you give it, even though you feel no immediate peace or joy. Belief at the outset is *trust*.

Your faith is so weak

But that does not matter, because nothing is said about the amount of one's faith. Because the word "believe" is so delightfully vague, the greatest faith could not make you more secure, and the smallest faith cannot put you outside the circle of God's blessing. Faith as a grain of mustard seed can move a mountain equally as faith as a walnut shell can.

You are not sure if you have the right faith

But all faith, any faith, is the right faith, if it is in Christ. There are not many sorts of faith. The faith that can only lay down its weary weight on Jesus; the faith that *tries* to look to Him; the faith that staggers toward Him and drops into His arms; the faith that cannot cling because its hands are so weak but

19

which calls to Him, believing that He can save—that is all the faith you need. And exercising it, you are saved.

You do not feel saved

Who said that feeling saved was an essential condition of salvation? Remember that it is one thing to be saved, and quite another to feel it. The one may exist without the other. The moment you look to Jesus you are saved, whether you feel it or not. Don't think about your feelings. Don't think about your faith. Look to Jesus, and reckon that God will keep His word and save you.

The result of all this must inevitably be peace. Faith simply turns to the Word of God and puts its finger on one of His exceedingly great and precious promises, saying, "This must fail before I can perish: 'I know whom I have believed and am persuaded that He is able to keep what I have committed to Him until that Day'" (see 2 Timothy 1:12).

THE SECRET OF PEACE IS CONSTANTLY REFERENCING THE CARE OF GOD

"Be anxious for nothing, but in everything by prayer and supplication, with thanksgiving, let your requests be made known to God; and the peace of God, which surpasses all understanding, will guard your hearts and your minds through Christ Jesus" (Phil. 4:6-7). Acid dropped on steel and allowed to remain there will soon corrode it. If we allow worries and anxieties to brood in our hearts, they will soon break up our peace just as swarms of tiny gnats will make a paradise uninhabitable.

There is only one thing to do. We must hand worries and anxieties over to Jesus as soon as they occur. It will not do to wait until the day is over, but in the midst of its busy rush, whenever we are conscious of having lost our peace, we should stop what we are doing and ask ourselves why, then lift up our hearts and pass it off into the care of our loving and compassionate Lord.

> "'TIS ENOUGH THAT
> HE SHOULD CARE,
> WHY SHOULD WE THE
> THE BURDEN BEAR?"

Ah! If only we could acquire this blessed habit! We look so weighted and lead such burdened lives because we do not trust Jesus with all the little worries of daily life. There is nothing small to Him if it hinders our peace. And when once you have handed anything to Him, refuse to take it back again, and treat the tendency to do so as a temptation to which you dare not give way, no, not for a moment.

Cares and concerns come from many sources. Our daily needs, our dear ones, our worldly prospects, our Christian ministry, our pathway in life, our spiritual growth—all these contribute their quota to the total sum. Let us take them all, lay them down at Jesus' feet, and leave them there. Then live, looking to Him to do in us, with us, through us, for us, just as He will. And as we give Him our cares, He will give us His peace; and as He does so He will whisper, "My peace I give to you. . . . Let not your heart be troubled, neither let it be afraid" (John 14:27).

There is a remarkable text in Isaiah 9:7 which predicts that the government of God's kingdom will be shouldered by the One we know as the Lord Jesus Christ, and that when it happens there will be no end to the increase of peace. When we take the principle here and apply it to the individual life as well, it has searching implications. Where is the government of our lives? Is it in our own hands? If so, we must not be surprised if our hearts are like the troubled sea when it cannot rest. There can be no peace, because there is perpetual clashing and rebellion. We are out of harmony with God and His will, which must be done—whether in us or in spite of us.

But as soon as we put the government of our lives—down to their smallest details—into the hands of the Lord Jesus, then we enter into His own infinite peace (cf. Col. 3:15). And when His government is extended over our hearts and lives, so does our peace extend, as when the blessed light of dawn spreads like a benediction over the world. "In Me you may have peace." It was our Savior who said those words. Let us abide in Him. Let us live in Him. Let us walk in Him. Let us make of Him the secret place to which we may continually go. And as we are joined to Him in the intimacy of deepest union, the peace that fills His heart, like a serenely placid ocean, shall begin to flow into ours until they are filled with the very fullness of God. The peace of God, like a fluttering dove, will settle upon our hearts and make them its home forevermore.

That this peace may become the blessed portion of you, my reader, is my sincere wish.

HOW TO
BEAR SORROW

You are passing through a time of deep sorrow. The love on which you were trusting has suddenly failed and dried up like a brook in the desert—now a dwindling stream, then shallow pools, and, at last, drought. You find yourself listening for footsteps that do not come, waiting for a word that is not spoken, pining for a reply that is long overdue.

Perhaps your financial savings have

suddenly disappeared; instead of helping others, you must be helped. Or you must leave the warm nest where you have been sheltered from life's storms to go alone into an unfriendly world. Or you are suddenly called to assume the burden of some other life, taking no rest for yourself till you have steered it through dark and difficult seas into the haven. Your health, sight, or energy is failing; you carry in yourself the sentence of death; the anguish of anticipating the future is almost unbearable. In other cases there is the sense of recent loss through death, like the gap in the forest-glade where the woodsman has lately been felling trees.

At such times, life seems almost insupportable. Will every day be as long as this? Will the slow-moving hours ever again increase their pace? Will life ever wrap itself in anything other than the torn autumn remnants of past summer glory?

Has God forgotten to be gracious? Has He

in anger shut up His tender mercies? Is His mercy gone forever?

THIS ROAD HAS BEEN TRODDEN BY MANY

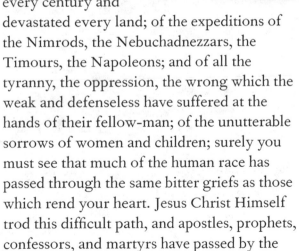

Think of the desolating wars that have swept through every century and devastated every land; of the expeditions of the Nimrods, the Nebuchadnezzars, the Timours, the Napoleons; and of all the tyranny, the oppression, the wrong which the weak and defenseless have suffered at the hands of their fellow-man; of the unutterable sorrows of women and children; surely you must see that much of the human race has passed through the same bitter griefs as those which rend your heart. Jesus Christ Himself trod this difficult path, and apostles, prophets, confessors, and martyrs have passed by the

29

same way. It is comforting to know that others have traveled the same dark valley. Where they were, we are. And, by God's grace, where they are now, we shall be.

Do Not Talk About Punishment

You may talk of chastisement or correction, for our Father does deal with us as with sons. You may speak of reaping the results of mistakes and sins dropped as seeds into life's furrows in former years. You may have to bear the consequences of the sins and mistakes of others; but do not speak of punishment. Surely all the guilt and penalty of sin was laid on Jesus, and He put them away forever. His were the stripes and the chastisement of our peace. If God punishes us for our sins, it would seem that the sufferings of Christ were incomplete; and if He once began to punish us, life would be too short for the infliction of all that we deserve.

Besides, how could we explain the anomalies of life and the heavy sufferings of the saints as compared with the pleasure-driven lives of the ungodly? Surely, if our sufferings were penal, there would be a reversal of these lots.

SORROW IS A REFINER'S CRUCIBLE

It may be caused by the neglect or cruelty of another, by circumstances over which the sufferer has no control, or as the direct result of some dark hour in the long past. But, inasmuch as God has permitted it to come, it must be accepted as His appointment. It must be considered as the furnace by which He is searching, testing, probing, and purifying the soul. Suffering searches us as fire does metals. We think we are fully for God until we are exposed to the cleansing fire of pain. Then we discover, as Job did, how much dross there is in us, and how little real patience, yieldedness, and faith. Nothing so detaches

31

us from the things of this world and the enticement of earthly affections as sorrow will. There is probably no other way by which the power of the self-life can be arrested so that the life of Jesus may be manifested in our mortal flesh.

GOD ALWAYS KEEPS THE DISCIPLINE OF SORROW IN HIS OWN HANDS

Our Lord said, "My Father is the vine-dresser." His hand holds the pruning-knife; His eye watches the crucible; His gentle touch is on the pulse while the operation is in progress. He will not allow even the devil to have his own way with us. As in the case of Job, so always. The moments are carefully allotted. The severity of the test is exactly determined by the reserves of grace and strength which are lying unrecognized within, but will be sought for and used beneath the severe pressure of pain. He dare not risk the loss of that which cost Him the blood of His Son. "God is faithful, who will not allow you to be tempted [tested] beyond what you are able, but with the temptation will also make the way of escape, that you may be able to bear [endure] it" (1 Cor. 10:13).

> GOD IS FAITHFUL, WHO WILL NOT ALLOW YOU TO BE TEMPTED BEYOND WHAT YOU ARE ABLE...

IN SORROW, THE COMFORTER IS NEAR

"GOD is . . . a very present help in trouble" (Ps. 46:1). He sits by the crucible, as a refiner of silver, regulating the heat, marking every change, waiting patiently for the scum to float away and His own face to be mirrored in clear, translucent metal. No earthly friend may tread the winepress with you, but the Savior is there, His garments stained with the blood of the grapes of your sorrow. Dare to repeat often, though you do not feel it, and though Satan insists that God has left you, *"You are with me."* Mention His name again and again: *"Jesus,* JESUS, You are with me." So you will become conscious that He is there.

When friends come to console you they talk of time's healing touch, as though the best balm for sorrow were to forget. Or in their well-meant kindness they suggest travel, diversion, amusement, and show their inability to appreciate the black night that hangs over your soul. So you turn from them, sick at heart and prepared to say, as Job did of his, "Miserable comforters are you all." But all the while Jesus is nearer than they are, understanding how they affect you, knowing each throb of pain, touched by fellow-feeling, silent in a love too full to speak, waiting to comfort from hour to hour as a mother does her weary, suffering baby.

Be sure to study the art of this divine comfort, so that you may be able to comfort others who are in trouble with the comfort with which you yourself have been comforted by God (see 2 Cor. 1:4). There can be no doubt that some trials are permitted to come to us, as to our Lord, for no other reason than that by means of them we should become able to empathize with and help others. And we should watch with all care each symptom of the pain and each prescription of the Great Physician, since in all probability at some future time we shall be called to minister to those passing through similar experiences. Thus we learn by the things that we suffer and, being made perfect, become authors of priceless and eternal help to souls in agony.

Do Not Shut Yourself Up With Your Sorrow

A friend, in the first anguish of bereavement, wrote, saying that he must

35

give up the Christian ministries in which he had been involved. I replied immediately, urging him not to do so, because there is no solace for heart-pain like ministry. The temptation of great suffering is toward isolation, withdrawing from social interaction, sitting alone, and keeping silence. Do not yield to it. Break through the icy chains of reserve if they have already gathered. Arise, wash your face and go forth to do your duty, with willing though chastened steps.

Selfishness of every kind, whether in its activities or its introspection, is hurtful. It shuts out the help and love of God. Sorrow is apt to be selfish. The soul, occupied with its own grief and refusing to be comforted, becomes presently like the Dead Sea, full of brine and salt, over which no birds fly and beside which no green thing grows. And thus we miss the very lesson that God would teach us. His constant war is against the self-life, and every pain He inflicts is to lessen its hold on us. We must beware of thwarting His purpose by extracting poison from His gifts, just as men gather drugs and alcohol from innocent plants.

A Hindu woman, so an eastern legend tells us, lost her only child. Wild with grief, she implored a prophet to return her little one to her. He looked at her tenderly for a long while, and said, "Go, my daughter, bring me a handful of rice from a house into which death has never entered, and I will do as you wish." The woman at once began her search. She went from house to house, and as far and wide as she wandered, there was always some vacant seat by the hearth. Gradually, the narrator says, the waves of her grief subsided before the spectacle of sorrow everywhere, and her heart, ceasing to be occupied with its own selfish pang, flowed out in strong yearnings of sympathy with the universal suffering. Tears of anguish softened into tears of pity. Passion melted

37

away in compassion. She forgot herself in the
general interest, and found redemption in
redeeming.

DO NOT CHIDE YOURSELF FOR FEELING STRONGLY

Tears are natural.
After all, Jesus wept.
A thunderstorm with-
out rain spells danger.
When rain does fall, not
only does it cool the air,
it relieves the overcharged
atmosphere. The swollen brooks
indicate that the snows are melting on the
hills and spring is near. "Daughters of
Jerusalem," said our Lord, "weep for
yourselves and for your children." To bear
sorrow with dry eyes and stolid heart may
befit a Stoic, but not a Christian. We have no
need to rebuke fond nature that cries for its
mate, for its lost joy, for the touch of the

vanished hand, for the sound of the voice that is still, provided only that the will is resigned. This is the one consideration for those who suffer— *Is the will right?* If it isn't, God Himself cannot comfort. If it is, then the path will inevitably lead from the valley of the shadow of death to the banqueting table and the overflowing cup.

Many say, "I cannot feel resigned. It is bad enough to have my grief to bear, but I have this added trouble, that I cannot *feel* resigned." My invariable reply is: you probably never can feel resignation, but you can *will* it. The Lord Jesus, in the Garden of Gethsemane, has shown us how to suffer. He chose His Father's will. Although Judas, prompted by Satan, was the instrument for mixing the cup and placing it to the Savior's lips, He looked right beyond him to the Father, who permitted him to work his cruel way, and said: "Shall I not drink the cup which My Father has given me?" And He said repeatedly, "If this cup cannot pass away from Me, unless I drink it, Your will be done." He gave up His own way and will, saying, "Not as I will, but as You will."

Let all sufferers who read these lines go somewhere quiet and dare to say the same words: "Your will, and not mine; Your will be done in the earth of my life, as in the heaven of Your purpose. I choose Your will." Say this thoughtfully and deliberately, not because you can feel it, but because you will it; not because the way of the cross is pleasant, but because it must be right. Say it repeatedly, whenever the surge of pain sweeps through you, whenever the wound begins to bleed afresh. Not my will, but Yours, be done. *Dare to say yes to God.* "Even so, Father, for so it seems good in Your sight."

> DARE TO
> SAY YES
> TO GOD.

And so you will be led to feel that all is right and well. And a great calm will settle down on your heart, a peace that passes understanding, a sense of rest which is not inconsistent with suffering but which walks in the midst of it, as the three young men experienced in the fiery furnace to whom the burning coals must have been like the dewy grass of a forest-glade.

BE SURE TO LEARN GOD'S LESSONS

Each sorrow carries at its heart a germ of holy truth, which if you sow in the soil of your heart will bear a harvest. God has a meaning in each blow of His chisel, each incision of His knife. But although His plan is perfect, His purposes are not always clear to us.

In suffering and sorrow God touches the

minor chords, develops the passive virtues, and opens to view the treasures of darkness, the constellations of promise, the rainbow of hope, the silver light of the covenant. What is character without sympathy, what are submission, patience, trust, and hope that grips the unseen as an anchor? These graces are only possible through sorrow. Sorrow is a garden, the trees of which are laden with the peaceable fruits of righteousness. Do not leave it without bringing them with you. Sorrow is a mine, the walls of which glisten with precious stones. Be sure you don't retrace your steps into daylight without some of these jewels. Sorrow is a school. You are sent to sit on its hard benches and learn lessons from it that will make you wise forever. Do not trifle away your chance of graduating there.

COUNT ON THE AFTERWARD

God will not always be causing grief. He

traverses the dull brown acres with His plough, cultivating the ground that He may be able to cast in the precious grain. Believe that in days of sorrow He is sowing light for the righteous and gladness for the upright in heart. Look forward to the reaping. Anticipate the joy which is set before you and which will flood your heart with joy when patience has completed her perfect work.

You will live to recognize the wisdom of God's choice for you. You will one day see that the thing you wanted was only second best. You will be surprised to remember that you once nearly broke your heart for what would never have satisfied you if you had caught it, just like the child chasing the butterfly or soap bubble. You will become possessed of a depth of character, a breadth of sympathy, a fund of patience, an ability to understand and help others which, as you lay them at Christ's feet for Him to use, will make you glad that you were afflicted. You will see God's plan and purpose; you will reap His harvest; you will behold His face and be satisfied. Each wound will have its pearl, each carcass will contain a swarm of bees, each foe, like Midian to Gideon, will yield its goodly spoil.

The way of the cross, rightly borne, is the only way to the everlasting light. The path that threads the Garden of Gethsemane and climbs over the hill of Calvary alone conducts us to the visions of the Easter morning and the glories of the ascension mount. If we will not drink of His cup, or be baptized with His baptism, or fill up that which is lacking in Christ's afflictions, we cannot expect to share in the joy and ecstasy of His triumph. But if these conditions are fulfilled, we shall not miss one note in the everlasting song, one element in the bliss that is available to all His children.

REMEMBER THAT
SUFFERING RIGHTLY
BORNE ENRICHES MANKIND

The death of Hallam was the birthday of Tennyson's *In Memoriam*. The cloud of insanity that brooded over Cowper gave us the hymn, "God moves in a mysterious way." Milton's blindness taught him to sing of "Holy Light, offspring of heaven's firstborn." Hymn writer Johann Rist used to say, "The dear cross has pressed many songs out of me." And it is probable that none rightly suffer anywhere without contributing something to the alleviation of human grief, to the triumph of good over evil, love over hate, and light over darkness.

If you believed this, could you not bear to suffer? Is not the chief misery of all suffering its loneliness, and perhaps its apparent pointlessness? Then dare to believe that no man dies to himself. Fall into the ground,

bravely and cheerfully, to die. If you refuse
this, you will abide alone, but if you yield to
it, you will bear fruit which will sweeten the
lot and strengthen the life of
others who may never
know your name or
stop to thank you
for your help.

Three

THE
BLESSED DEAD

*O*n a seaside dock of an obscure Norwegian town I once saw a parting between a little group of emigrants who were about to try their fortunes in a strange and distant land. Their friends and relatives had gathered to bid them a last goodbye. They were all of the poorest class, their goods in a handful of clumsy boxes, and their mutual grief was evident. The main point of my interest,

however, was the wistful eager-
ness with which the eyes of
those on the shore followed
the wake of the retreating
vessel, as though they might
possibly pierce the parting
veil of distance and see the
land their dear ones were
going to, perhaps never to return.
So it is often as we gather around the spot
from which some beloved soul is about to
depart into the unseen. Where does the soul
go? What does it behold? What's the origin of
the light that illuminates the tired features till
they seem already transfigured into the
likeness of the immortal? We gaze where we
almost expect to see an open heaven, but all is
opaque and dark. And we turn away to take
up our lonely path and to wonder with a great
awe as to what is really involved in this great
and solemn mystery which we call death, but
which angels know as birth.

Obviously, in death, there is no break in the soul's consciousness. The life of the spirit is altogether independent of the body in which it dwells. The signal-box may be in ruins, and yet the operator may be within—as clear in thought and quick of hand as in the day when all was new. It often happens, when the body is at the point of death, that the spirit reveals itself in undiminished splendor and flashes forth in thoughts that can never be forgotten and in words that can never die. And does not this prove beyond doubt that the spirit is only a lodger in the body, and that when the form of its tabernacle is broken up it is not affected but simply passes out to find some other and more lasting home? "We know that if our earthly house, this tent [this bodily frame] is destroyed, we have a building from God, a house not made with hands, eternal in the heavens" (2 Cor. 5:1).

This conclusion, arrived at on merely natural and logical grounds, is substantiated by the New Testament. There is no support for the idea held by some that there is a pause in our consciousness, a parenthesis in our existence, between death and the resurrection. "To depart," said the apostle Paul, is to "be with Christ, which is far better" (Phil. 1:23). Better to live on in this mortal life, amid the acutest sufferings, and to have the presence of Christ, than to lose that presence during centuries of unconsciousness.

"To be absent from the body," Paul said again, is "to be present with the Lord" (2 Cor. 5:8). The moment of absence is the moment of presence. As the spirit withdraws itself from the body, closing blinds and shutters as it retires, it immediately presents itself in the presence of the Savior, never to depart.

"God will bring with Him those who sleep in Jesus" (that is, with the Lord at His second coming for His own). "And the dead in Christ will rise first" (1 Thess. 4:14, 16). Clearly, then, those who have "fallen asleep in Jesus" (this being the constant phrase used in the Scriptures for the death of the believer) have gone to be with Christ, or they could not be said to return with Him. And their spirit-life must be independent of their bodies, which will only be raised when the angel trumpet calls them from the grave.

The apostle John distinctly closes the door against all further doubt and questioning on this matter when he says, "I heard a voice from heaven saying to me, 'Write: Blessed are the dead who die in the Lord from now on'" (Rev. 14:13). What can these last words mean, except that the blessed rest of the beloved dead dates from the moment that they died in the Lord.

Death is not a state, but an act; not a condition, but a passage. In this it finds its true analogy in birth, by which we entered upon a new stage of existence. In death we are born out of the darkness and constraints of this mortal life into the freedom and light of heaven. So Christ was called "the firstborn from the dead." A moment's anguish; a wrench; a step; a transition; a breaking through the thin veil which hangs between two worlds; a stepping across the boundary line—such is death. And the soul carries with it across that boundary line its freight of thought and life to pursue its continuity of being and love and purpose in an unbroken and uninterrupted course. The dead are those who have died and are living forevermore an intense, bright life (Ps. 21:6).

Their love to us was a part of their existence, woven into their innermost being. It was not a property of the body that they have left behind, but of themselves. And we cannot think of them as being the same beings as they were without that love. If, as

we have seen, the spirit carries on its life unbroken and unaffected by its passage from the
body, then it must continue to live on the other
side as on this side. Its love is only
altered in its brilliance and intensity,
not in its objects, just as a piece of
phosphorus, which burns in
ordinary air but sparkles and flashes
when suddenly plunged into a jar of
oxygen gas.

> LOVE
> ABIDES
> FOREVER.

Love never dies (1 Cor. 13:13). Our partial
knowledge dies amid the revelations of perfect
vision. *Faith* will be needed no more where we
know as we are known. *Hope* fades in fruition.
But *love* abides forever. It never fails. Death
may cut off the interchange of words and acts
of love, but its cold hand cannot touch that
which is divine in origin, eternal in nature, and
everlasting in duration.

That is what we yearn to know. It is not
the distance that makes our souls faint and
fear—we could bear that—but the feeling that

perhaps we have lost forever the love which
was the light of our
existence, the fire
at which we were
accustomed to
warming
ourselves. Let us
know that this
is preserved to
us still; that they
love us still who
have left us; that their thoughts still enfold us
in tender embrace, follow us in our
wanderings, and hover over us like
ministering angels—then we can afford to be
without their presence. No, we gladly resign
them, because they are happier where they
are than we could ever have made them.

If your child were to cross the seas and
sojourn for all coming years of life amid
strange surroundings and foreign tongues,
would you expect him to cease to love you?

Did Joseph forget his father or brothers when suffering in the prison or reigning on the throne? Did Moses cease to love his mother when for forty years he dwelt in the palace of the pharaohs? Did the little maid forget her home when she was transported to the halls of the warrior Naaman? And why should we suppose that those forget us who have passed into the City of God, where the soul only loses its grossness and denseness, but where all that is true and noble and lovely reveals itself in fellowship with its fellows?

O press this thought to your innermost soul: that those whom you have loved long since and lost awhile love you still with a warmth of affection that kindles into an intense brilliance as they come nearer to the heart of the Eternal Father, the source and sun of love. And in this love they wait for us. They cannot attain their full consummation and bliss until we, too, emerge

...IN THIS LOVE THEY WAIT FOR US

from the shadows of death into the perfect light of eternity. Only then shall love be satisfied.

But if the love of earth be preserved on the other side, will they not suffer more pain than pleasure, more anguish for those who are overcome by evil than joy for those who conquer? Yet surely heaven cannot be a place of selfish enjoyment! The very essence of its bliss will be in thought and care for others. Its happy residents cannot be oblivious to the travail that rends the heart of its Master for the world He loves and for the church, His bride. Death will only bring them into closer sympathy with Him in His great plans of redemption, and may reveal to them considerations and possibilities that will mitigate their anxiety, enabling them to await the unfolding of His plans for those whom they have left behind.

Our sainted dead will be capable of recognition. Of what use would it be if they were so changed that we could not know them? Even if they were the same in essence, they would not be the same to us. Of course, they will not wear the body of mortality, racked with pain, dissolved in death. "Flesh and blood cannot inherit the kingdom of God. . . . This corruptible must put on incorruption, and this mortal must put on immortality" (1 Cor. 15:50, 53). But the resurrection body, as is proved by the testimony of those who saw Christ in the days before He ascended to the Father, though in many respects different, is so nearly like the body of our present life that it can be recognized—not only in the general outline, but by the very intonation of the voice that speaks the dear old familiar names of the past. Mary did not recognize Christ at first because she would not lift her tear-blinded eyes from the grave where she had seen His sacred body laid. But the tones of His voice recalled her from her sad reverie and prompted her to recognize Him. The two who walked to Emmaus would have known Him if their eyes had not been kept from recognizing Him. And when repeated opportunities were given to the rest of the disciples to verify Him as the same Jesus with whom they had spent three years of blessed fellowship, they knew Him and "were glad when they saw the Lord." The ones who did not see Him were those whose senses were clouded by unbelief or earthliness.

So shall it be with all who belong to Him. His resurrection body is a pattern of ours. The Lord Jesus Christ "will transform our lowly body that it may be conformed to His glorious body" (Phil. 3:21). The spirit will be robed in a spiritual body, obedient to its every bidding, the suitable vehicle of its bright and blessed life. But that glorious body will, in its tones, look, and acts (John 21:7), recall the loved spirit with which our heart was entwined.

Sometimes, when reaching our destination, we have been refreshed by seeing

the faces of those we know and love who
have come to meet us.
This is how Paul
felt as his weary
journey approached
its end at Appii-Forum
(Acts 28:15). But what
joy it will be to be greeted
on the other side by familiar faces, well-
known voices, and tokens by which to
recognize the dearly loved! Yet this is what
we may expect. We are to be gathered unto
our people, a phrase which cannot mean their
dust, because the word "buried" is used of
this, meaning, therefore, their living, loving,
recognized, and welcoming presence. Those
whom we have befriended will welcome us
into eternal habitation. A choral entrance is
to be ministered unto us into the home of the
saints (Luke 16:9; 2 Peter 1:11).

Once more: The blessed dead are not far
away. They are where Jesus is; and since He

is here, may they not be here too? Heaven is
not far away, but near at hand, within the
moment's flash of the spirit's flight. "Today"
(and it was near sunset when Jesus said it to
the penitent thief on the cross), "you will be
with Me in Paradise." Absent from the body,
present with the Lord. No doubt there are
several heavens through which, ultimately,
spirits will pass in their upward mounting
(Eph. 4:10). But the third chamber of the
many mansions, Paradise, where the blessed
dead are now gathering and where they await
the resurrection, is near, very near (2 Cor.
12:2, 4). There is but a step between.

The prayer of Jesus was that His church
should be one in the Father and Himself. He
made no distinction between those who
should have crossed the borderline and those
still lingering on this side. And thus we may
infer that all those who are one with Him are
one with each other; and that, when we
realize our union with Him most closely, we

also realize our union with all believers in
heaven and earth, and especially with our
beloved. Moses and Elijah met the disciples
on the Mount of Transfiguration. And saints
still meet us when we are nearest Christ. The
members of the same body cannot be very
far from each other!

Those
distanced by
miles of land
and sea meet each
other in spirit as they
gather at the same hour
to remember the Lord; and
those who touch Christ from
the heaven-side meet us in Him
when we touch Him from the earth-side.
Hallelujah! To the holy soul, not heaven
only, but earth and vale and hill and lovely
scenes are thronged with the presence of
bright, radiant, and holy spirits, among
whom we recognize those who have been

ours, and are ours, forever.

And there is this thought also for those who have lost a child, the bright dear life from which it seemed so hard to part. From the moment that death takes them, they cease to grow old; they always remain to us what they were in all their sweet innocence. There is always a child-life in the house where a child has died, always merry ringing tones, always soft caresses, always pretty childish ways. The other children grow up and pass out into life and the world, but the child whom death has taken is always there. O death, you angel of God, you seem to rob us of our treasures, but really you make them ours forever in the dew of an immortal youth, transfiguring them with a light that can never fade from their faces or from our lives, blotting out only what we are glad to forget, and preserving what we loved in imperishable beauty.

The bereaved have often said to me bitterly, "I cannot *feel* resigned; I know that it

must be all right, but I cannot *feel* resigned."
But does God expect us to deny the love He
gave us, pining, as it does, for the touch of
the vanished hand and the sound of the voice
that is still? Remember: Jesus wept at the
grave of His friend.

There are two kinds of sorrow. There is
the sorrow which misses its companion at
every turn and which at each fresh sense of
loss weeps bitter tears under a keen sense of
pain. And there is the hard, bitter and
unsubmissive sorrow which will not forgive
God. It is only the latter of these that is
wrong. The first is natural, and
there is no cause in it for self-
rebuke.

When grief is fresh do not
try to feel resignation; rather,
will it. Look up to God, in the
first stab of pain, and in all the
long weary hours of suffering
which follow, and say, "Father,

WHEN GRIEF
IS FRESH DO
NOT TRY
TO FEEL
RESIGNATION;
RATHER,
WILL IT.

I choose Your will; I know it is the tenderest and best for my loved one, and for me. Because it seemed good in Your sight, Father, I say, 'not my will, but Yours, be done.'" And as these words are repeated, and the will offers itself to God and lays its sacrifice upon the altar, though the hand trembles and the eyes brim with tears, the inward agitation will subside and die down, and the sufferer will come to delight, not in the sorrow, but in the Father's appointment, which at first it could only *choose*.

We never know from what lingering suffering, from what bitter grief, from what impending disaster, spiritual or temporal, God has taken our dear ones. He knows best. He has a sufficient reason and will explain it clearly to us some day. Meanwhile, He who wounds can heal. He who takes will Himself fill the vacant place.

God sometimes leads us into the valley of shadow that we may learn the way and know

how to lead others through it into the light.
To get comfort we must comfort with the
comfort wherewith we ourselves have been
comforted. In wiping the tears of others, our
own will cease to fall.

Four

COMFORTED TO COMFORT

*B*lessed be the God and Father of our Lord Jesus Christ, the Father of mercies and God of all comfort, who comforts us in all our tribulation, that we may be able to comfort those who are in any trouble, with the comfort with which we ourselves are comforted by God" (2 Cor. 1:3-4).

Child of God, think it not strange concerning the fiery trial that tries you, as though some strange thing has happened. Rejoice, because it is a sure sign that you are on the right track.

In an unknown country, a man tells me that I shall presently pass over a stony bit of road on the way to my destination, and when I come to it, each jolt tells me that I am on the right road. So when a child of God passes through affliction, he is not surprised, but satisfied, for he knows that it is through much tribulation that we enter the kingdom. Your afflictions cannot be few.

Look Up

There is your Father, pure and holy. You

are to be like Him. But before you can be like Him, you will need the heat of the crucible— not to earn your way to heaven, but to destroy your unheavenliness. The spirits gathered there tell you that the brilliance of their reward has been in the measure of the severity of their sorrows. Be sure, then, that your Father will put within your reach a brighter crown by putting you within the reach of severe affliction.

Look Down

Do you think that the prince of hell was pleased when you forsook him for your new Master, Christ? Of course not! At the moment of your conversion, all the powers of darkness pledged themselves to obstruct your way. Do not be surprised if affliction comes to you, as it came to Job, by the permission of heaven, from hell!

Look Around

You are still in the world that crucified your Lord, and would do the same again if He were once more to live in it. It cannot love you. It will cast you out of its synagogue. It will think it a religious act to kill you. In the world you shall have afflictions, though in the midst of them you may be of good cheer.

> IN THE WORLD YOU SHALL HAVE AFFLICTIONS, THOUGH IN THE MIDST OF THEM YOU MAY BE OF GOOD CHEER.

Look Within

Your heart is evil in nature, ever chafing against the rule and will of God—disobedient, restless, willful. And in the constant strife between your will and God's will, what can there be but affliction? This human life is the college of affliction, where even the King's Son came that He might be a faithful High Priest, touched with the feelings of our infirmities.

For such as you are, afflicted one, there is no literature so befitting as the Bible, and in the Bible no part more helpful than the Second Epistle to the Corinthians. *Hope* is the keynote of the epistle to the Thessalonians; *joy* of that to the Philippians; *faith* of that to the Romans; *heavenly things* of that to the Ephesians; *affliction* of this one. It was written amid afflictions so great that the apostle despaired of life. It is steeped in affliction, as a handkerchief with the flowing blood of a fresh wound. But in this passage the apostle has built for himself a little chamber of comfort on the wall of affliction. Its stones are quarried from the pit of his own sorrow. In it he sits and sings, "Blessed be God," and into it he bids you come till your affliction be past and your sky is clear again. It is the chamber of comfort.

When in affliction, mind three things— look out for comfort, store up comfort, and pass on the comfort you receive.

LOOK OUT FOR COMFORT

It will come *certainly*.
Wherever the nettle grows,
there grows the dock
leaf. And wherever
there is a trial, there is,
somewhere at hand, a
sufficient store of
comfort, though our
eyes, like Hagar's, are
often kept from seeing
it. But it is as sure as the
faithfulness of God.

It will come *proportionately*. God holds a pair
of scales. This on the right side is for your
afflictions; this on the left side is for your comfort.
And the beam is always level. The more your
trial, the more your comfort. As the sufferings of
Christ abound in us, so our consolation also
abounds through Christ.

It will come *divinely*. It is good to know in what quarter to look for comfort. Shall we look to the hills? No, for in vain is salvation found in the hills. Shall we look to man? No, for Job found the best men of his time to be miserable comforters. Shall we look to angels? No. God trusts angels to fulfill many ministries for us, but never to comfort. This needs a gentler touch than theirs. It is *He* who comforts those that are cast down. It is *He* who heals the broken in heart and binds up their wounds.

It will come *through a mediator*. Our consolation abounds *through Christ*. When a bridegroom presents a gift to his beloved, he may package it carefully and send it by her closest friend. And when our God comforts us, He adds to the exquisite beauty of His comfort by sending it through the Son of His love.

It will come *directly* through the Holy Spirit, that other Comforter, whom the Savior gives, and who gives us Him, and in giving us Him, gives us all.

It will come *in various forms*, sometimes by the coming of a beloved Titus; sometimes in the form of a bouquet, a letter, a message, or a card; sometimes by a promise, laying an ice-cold cloth on our fevered brows; sometimes by God simply coming near. In sore sorrow, he comforts best who says least and who simply draws near, takes the sufferer's hand, and is silent in his sympathizing love. It is *so* that God comforts. You drew near in the day of my affliction; You said, "It is I, be not afraid."

Store Up Comfort

The world is full of comfortless hearts, orphan children crying in the night. Our God pities them, and He would comfort them through you. But before you are sufficient for this lofty ministry, you must be trained. And that He may train you perfectly, He puts you through the very same afflictions that are wringing human hearts with aching sorrow. He makes thus for Himself an opportunity of comforting you and of so teaching you the divine art of comfort. Watch narrowly how He does it. Keep a diary and note down all the procedure of His skill. Ponder in your heart the length of each splint, the folds of each bandage, the ministration of each sedative or drug. This will bring a twofold blessing. It will turn your thoughts from your miseries to your outnumbering mercies; and it will take from you that sense of useless and aimless existence that is often the sufferer's weariest cross.

Do you wonder why you suffer some special form of sorrow? Wait, till ten years are past. I warrant you that in that time you will find some, perhaps ten, afflicted as you are.

Do you
WONDER
WHY YOU
SUFFER
SOME
SPECIAL
FORM OF
SORROW?

When you tell them how you have suffered and how you have been comforted—while you unfold your tale and seek to repeat on them the ways you have dealt with your griefs—in their glistening eyes and comforted looks you will learn why you have been afflicted, and you will bless God that you were able to comfort others with the comfort wherewith you yourself have been comforted of God. Once more, then, remember to store up an accurate remembrance of the ways in which God comforts you.

PASS ON THE COMFORT YOU RECEIVE

At a railway station, a benevolent man found a schoolboy in tears because he had not quite enough to pay his fare, and he remembered how, years before, *he* had been in the same plight. He had been helped at the time by an unknown friend and had been exhorted to pass that kindness on to another person some day. Now he saw that the long-expected moment had come. He took the weeping boy aside, told him his story, paid his fare, and asked him, in his turn, to pass the kindness on. As the train moved from the station, the lad cried cheerily: "I will pass it on, sir!" So, the act of thoughtful love is continually being passed on from one person to another around the globe.

"Go and do likewise." Is your heart comforted? Then be on the alert to comfort those who are in any trouble. You cannot miss them; they are not scarce. Your own sad past will make you quick to detect them where others might miss them. If you do not find them, seek them; the wounded heart goes alone to die. Sorrow shuns society. You should constantly seek from the Man of Sorrows Himself directions as to where the sorrowing bide. He knows their haunts from which they have cried to Him. And when you learn where they are, do for them as the Good Samaritan did for you when He bound up *your* wounds, pouring in oil and wine. Comfort them with the comfort wherewith you yourself have been comforted of God.